HARBOR WANDERERS

A MICHIGAN BOATING EXPERIENCE

C.J. and Edna Elfont

Sleeping Bear Press
121 South Main
Chelsea, MI 48118
www.sleepingbearpress.com

Printed and bound in Canada by Friesen's, Altona, Manitoba.

10 9 8 7 6 5 4 3 2 1

Elfont, C.J.
Harbor wanderers: a Michigan boating experience / photography by C.J. Elfont & text by Edna Elfont.
p. cm.
ISBN 1-886947-19-8
1. Boats and boating--Michigan--Pictorial works. 2. Harbors--Michigan--Pictorial works. I. Elfont,
Edna A. II. Title. GV776.M5E43 1999
797.1'09774--DC21
98-50524
CIP

DEDICATION

This is dedicated to every boater whose enthusiasm, good humor, friendliness, and hospitality we were lucky enough to personally experience and to all those with whom we might have had similar experiences had our latitude and longitude been different.

We would like to extend special thanks to Dave Wallace for his encouragement, his editorial assistance, and his willingness to befriend two harbor wanderers.

On the cover: Harbor Beach
Title page: Grand Haven

FOREWORD

As it is with most serendipitous events, my chance encounter with C.J. and Edna Elfont quickly grew into a mutually supportive relationship. They were exploring selected Michigan ports of call that best supported the theme of this book...which was then in process. As a reference for helping them develop an itinerary, they chose to use the *Lakeland Boating Ports O' Call Cruising Guide for Lake Michigan*, which just happened to be my baby. As a token of gratitude for this ego-massaging vote of confidence in my own attempt at book authorship, I promptly bought a copy of their impressive book, *Sand Dunes of the Great Lakes*. From that moment on, we were bonded by the insecurities of creativity and shared pain that comes from pursuing the holy grail of acceptance by readers and book retailers alike.

Because we were both frequenting the same ports, our paths crossed often during the summer of 1997, and my respect for C.J.'s photo-stalking skills and Edna's poetic way with words grew with each new encounter. When I was finally invited to write the Foreword to this book, I jumped at the chance to be part of a work that I had watched so long in progress, and that illustrated so eloquently what the harbor experience is all about.

The boating lifestyle as lived on our seductive but volatile Great Lakes is a challenge of many over-lapping dimensions. In the decades that my wife and I have pursued cruising as our summer activity of choice, we still find that each season is an original, with an educational curriculum of its own. The process never stops. It is the incredible gamut of human emotions which are generated between the extremes of lonely open water and richly complex harbor life, that C.J. and Edna have captured on film and in words. If you too are a boater, parts of this book will resonate with your own experiences. If you are not...who knows?...this story may seduce you into a launching of your own.

Either way...welcome aboard!

Dave Wallace
Contributing Editor
Lakeland Boating Magazine

Lexington

INTRODUCTION

As a child I read stories of boats. They were tales of adventure, exploration, and people confronting natural forces they could not control. The stories were very different from each other, as stories usually are, but always there was excitement. And so it was, the first time I set foot on a boat. And so it has been each time since.

I have tried to understand why boating attracts so many people. Perhaps it is because boating is an experience that is always new and never totally predictable. Perhaps it is because boating takes us to places we can see no other way; places where land may be seen only as a distant object, if at all. Perhaps it is because on a boat there is a sense of freedom; freedom from roads and traffic jams and signs saying "Do Not Enter." Perhaps it is because aboard a boat, your everyday identity can be shed and you can feel closer to the adventurers and explorers that filled your childhood books.

But the pleasures of boating do not stop at the waters' edge. Just beyond the boat itself, the harbors await with their potpourri of pleasures. Harbors are much more than places to anchor a boat. They are places where old friends meet and new friends are made. They are vacation spots, places for entertainment and family gatherings, and places in which, for some brief time, we can change the pace and quality of our lives.

This book is a celebration of boats, boaters, and the harbors in which they congregate. With small brush strokes, C.J. and I have tried to create one canvas on which you will see and feel the part of boating that transforms a sport into a lifestyle. It is our hope that boaters from anywhere in the U.S. will open this book and, with but minor differences, see themselves, their friends, and their home ports. Perhaps they will see with new eyes a phase of the life they lead or they may simply be reminded of places visited and people once known.

Northport

Harbor Springs

When the great glaciers that covered a third of the earth's surface retreated for the final time, they left behind a vast freshwater lake with thousands of islands. Over the 9,500 years since the glaciers' last departure, that single lake has been transformed into five; five Great Lakes. These phenomenal bodies of water may be lakes to a geographer, but they do not look or act like lakes. Many refer to them as inland seas because they cover more than 94,000 square miles and contain one-fifth of all the earth's freshwater. It is to these inland seas that more recreational boaters than anywhere else in our country are drawn.

The shores of these lakes are graced with areas of phenomenal beauty. There are towering sand dunes strung like so many pearls along much of Lake Michigan's east coast. Although more scattered, there are dunes along the shores of all five lakes. The Great Lakes' dunes are the world's largest accumulation of sand dunes that border a body of freshwater. They are unique in both their origin and the multitude of environments that exist upon them. They are irreplaceable because the glacial forces that caused them to exist are long gone and are unlikely to return. These are not simply vast accumulations of sand, devoid of water and color. They are endowed not only with stretches of uninterrupted sand, but with beaches bordering freshwater lakes, fields of grasses and wildflowers, mature forests, ponds, swamps, and rivers. An area rich in contrasts, dense beech-maple forests are but steps away from vast stretches of sand bearing little more than sparse patches of pioneer grass. In addition to dunes, the shoreline is dotted with hardwood forests, stands of towering conifers, cedars and spruces, large stretches of orchid

9

and wildflower-rich marshes, and wetlands replete with waterfowl.

From childhood, we learn of the many dangers and terrible storms that can confront recreational boaters who venture onto any of the world's great seas. Except for the absence of sharks and other dangerous marine life, the potential hazards of the Great Lakes are much like those of any mighty ocean. Today, our boats have radar and other electronic devices to minimize these hazards, but no equipment can help when the waves are higher than your boat or crew can handle.

The Great Lakes are at the center of the North American weather system; a place meteorologists have called a "climatological battlefield." This is where air masses which normally come from the West collide with those from either the warm, humid Gulf of Mexico or the cold, dry Arctic. When these conflicting forces meet, anything can happen......and it often does. Change is frequent and can be sudden, resulting in the intrusion of fog and heavy rain or snow. What is already a complex weather system is further complicated by the unusual geographic relationship created by having large bodies of water surrounded by immense land masses. This intimate relationship of land and water, each having different temperatures, causes the movement of huge volumes of air powered by tremendous energy. The amount of energy released from the cooling of the warm lakes on but one autumn day is equal to one year's energy consumption in the U.S.! This means that boaters on the Great Lakes must be prepared for fast changing weather patterns. Although the worst storms tend to occur when recreational boaters have given up cruising in favor of their favorite chairs, the remote controls, and weekend football, the cruising months also have their share of rough weather. In shallow Lakes Huron and Erie, it does not take a lot of intense wind to churn ripples into high waves. Although Lake Huron is the second largest Great Lake, its

Charlevoix

Charlevoix

The wind
Stokes the furnace
That is the storm so the
Waters' flames light the sky with their
Fury.

Ludington

East Tawas

average depth is only 194 feet (not even one-half the depth of Lake Superior and about 30 percent more shallow than the average depth of Lake Michigan). So when winds of 22-24 knots came up during the first day of the 1997 Huron to Mackinaw race, waves of up to four feet resulted. These conditions presented unexpected problems and some emergency repairs for those participants who were unprepared. Typical of the drastic changes on the lake, the second day of racing saw breezes of only 2-4 knots, hardly enough to move a sailboat.

On the Great Lakes, wind alone can generate waves up to 7 feet even when no rainstorm is present. Lake Erie, with an average depth of only 62 feet, is the most shallow of the Great Lakes. Because of the shallow depth, winds actually push the water from one end of the lake to the other, producing high waves and large, short-term differences in the water levels at the lake's opposing ends.

The resemblance of the Great Lakes to the great seas does not end at wind and weather. Islands, whether in salt or fresh water, are likely to have shoals with hidden sandbars and barely visible rocks. Those of the Great Lakes are no exception. As early as 1818, what would eventually become a large network of lighthouses was started to protect commercial ships from these potentially fatal hazards.

And as on any ocean in the world, the recreational boater is not alone on the Great Lakes. On any one summer day, there may be 50 commercial ships just in the St. Clair River alone. (The St. Clair River leads from Lake Huron to Lake St. Clair which connects to Lake Erie via the Detroit River.) These ships, some of which measure up to 1,000 feet long and 105 feet wide, can carry up to 81,000 tons of iron ore; 75,000 barrels of heating oil; or 45,000 tons of coal, limestone, grain, potash, salt, or sand in one load. To put the size of these ships in perspective, the world's tallest building (the Sears tower in Chicago) is only 454 feet taller than these vessels are long.

The beauty and challenges of the Great Lakes draw millions of recreational boaters each year in spite of the short boating season. Boaters along the Great Lakes rarely put their boats into use much before mid-May and few leave them past early October. Only the hardiest begin mid-April, assuming the ice has melted. Fewer are foolhardy enough to risk the gales of November which have claimed the life of many a great ship. Perhaps the enthusiasm of Great Lakes boaters has something to do with the seven months they must spend looking forward to that first cruise. The moment that weather and work schedules allow, they exuberantly appear in large numbers.

For each of 14 years (1983 through 1996), more boats were registered in Michigan than in any other state. In 1996, there were 138,000 more boats registered in Michigan than in second place California and 203,000 more than third place Florida. Thirty-four percent of all boats registered in all 50 states in 1996 were registered in one of the states bordering a Great Lake (Illinois, Indiana, Michigan, Minnesota, New York, Ohio, Pennsylvania, and Wisconsin). Also, the waterway with the greatest concentration of small watercraft in the country is Lake St. Clair which lies between Lakes Erie and Huron, connecting to Lake Erie by the Detroit River and to Lake Huron by the St. Clair River.

Of the 50 states, none has more freshwater coastline than Michigan and only Alaska has a longer total coastline. With over 80 percent of its borders lying on the waters of four of the five Great Lakes, Michigan has 38,575 square miles of the Great Lakes and 3,000 islands of all sizes within its political boundaries. It is said that nowhere in Michigan are you more than 85 miles from one of the Great Lakes.

After World War II, it became evident that recreational boating was becoming a driving economic force in the Great Lakes. Although many boaters feel that the exhilaration of boating is diminished without some risk, it became necessary

Bay Harbor

Hammond Bay

to find some way of limiting that risk. Building new harbors was one such way. Michigan, in partnership with the U.S. Congress, responded by developing a "harbors of refuge" program. By definition, a harbor is a place where boats may find shelter or refuge. The expression *harbor of refuge* is not redundant however, because all harbors do not afford refuge to all boats. Many harbors are not deep enough for all boats, while others are simply not safe enough for anchoring recreational boats. Such harbors are only safe for small boats if appropriate dock space is provided. The harbors of refuge program's stated goal was to create enough protective harbors and marinas so that no recreational boater would ever be more than fifteen shoreline miles from safety. Although that goal has not yet been reached, as of this writing there are 87 recreational and state-commissioned harbors along Michigan's coastline and islands. Of those, 55 are on the mainland of the Lower Peninsula.

Because of all Michigan has to offer, many of the boaters in its harbors are from other states. Many not only cruise in Michigan waters, but rent slips in Michigan marinas and store their boats there in the off-season. In addition to their sheer numbers, Michigan's harbors of refuge offer widely varying environments, provide a wide range of diversions and services for boaters (especially in the Lower Peninsula), and have an exceptional sense of community. For these reasons, the images in this book were photographed in Michigan's Lower Peninsula. These images, however, are more about boats and boaters than the physical nature of the harbors. They are pieces of a jigsaw puzzle which collectively make up a picture of any Great Lakes harbor.

Ludington

Elk Rapids

Greilickville

Port Austin

The paint
Must be perfect
And the line must be straight
No less will do for this first boat
Of mine.

Muskegon

Beyond
Mathematics,
There are those among us
For whom one plus one
equals more
Than two.

Leland

White Lake

Tawas City

I *see*
Water and boats,
And brightly colored flags
And the artist paints a quiet
Garden.

Bay Harbor

New Buffalo

New Buffalo

South Haven

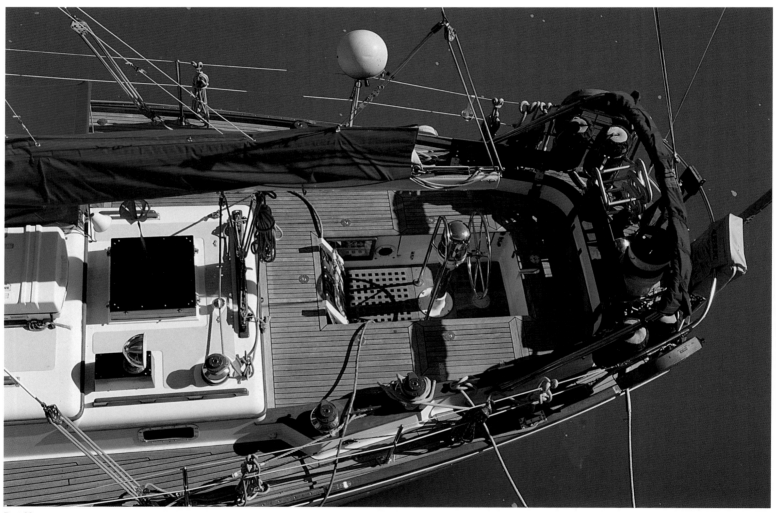

Port Huron

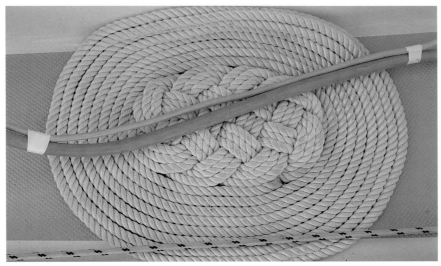

Holland

Elk Rapids

Elk Rapids

Pentwater

I will
Take any chance
To dally rather than
Forego the spectacle that is
Sunset.

Pentwater

Mackinaw City

Presque Isle

South Haven

Suttons Bay

New Buffalo

New Buffalo

Cheboygan

The one
Who is dressed in
The garb of command is
Not always the person who has
The control.

Saugatuck

Port Austin

Alpena

Harbor Beach

Leland

A safe
Harbor is our
Safety net when we dare
And a place of comfort when we
Dare not.

Leland

East Tawas

There is always a sense of anticipation when the moment comes to turn the boat toward a harbor. Of course, when running from bad weather, anxiety may surpass anticipation on the emotional scale. In calm waters, however, the first entry into a new harbor is always special, bringing with it a feeling of discovery. Even if the harbor is one previously visited, there is always a new experience waiting because the people and conditions are different each time. Some boaters have very clear expectations of what or whom they want to find in port while others are content with any new experience or simply the pleasant repetition of a familiar one.

The anticipation of entering a harbor usually initiates a flutter of activity on board the incoming boat. First, there is the cleanup; partially cosmetic to favorably impress shoreline onlookers and dock mates and partially practical to clear decks of anything that might interfere with docking. Cleaning and boat preparations over, crew members assume their necessary physical positions and preferred facial expressions for that critical moment when the boat enters the channel. The favored facial expressions are: serious but assured, benignly bored, cocky, or haughty. The crew must accomplish all this posturing while actually doing the job of docking, often under the scrutiny of a crowd of curious fellow cruisers already secure in their slips.

The real test of one's ability to maintain a look of confidence comes when bringing the boat into the slip. At some moment in time a crew member has to throw a line to someone standing on the dock. Some crew members hate this moment for, if this is not performed with the grace and efficiency of a big league pitcher, a heated discussion of the process may

Suttons Bay

Bay City

ensue between captain and crew member with each finding fault with the other's technique. This can be especially stressful if they happen to be spouses. If there is no one to catch the line, the test is harder. The captain must get the boat close enough to the dock for the crew member holding the line to jump to it without breaking any limbs. The crew member must make the leap quickly enough to fend off the boat and avoid the dreaded crunching of boat against dock. If the crew member is to impress onlookers, he/she has to make the jump with the agility of a gymnast wearing a blasé, I-can-do-this-blindfolded look on their face. And if a line must be tossed to lasso a piling, one must do it rodeo style if onlookers are to be at all impressed. Simply getting the line on the piling is not sufficient to gain kudos from the neighbors, but missing it is a sure way to entertain them. That they may be no more accomplished may not negate their amusement, but they are usually polite enough to refrain from pointing and snickering.

In spite of minor criticisms by one boater of another's skill, there is a common bond among boaters and it is born of shared experiences. Even owners of the largest boat have seen their share of terrible weather, docking mishaps, and failed engines. All boaters are the potential captives of weather, fuel, and pump-out requirements. (Pumping out of waste is required to comply with the federal regulations that prohibit the overboard discharge of untreated sewage within three miles of the coasts and anywhere on inland waters.) A boater rarely needs to ask for help, usually another boater offers it if there is simply the appearance of a problem.

The harbor is a conglomeration of people of different socioeconomic backgrounds, ages, and occupations who have at least one common interest and who all share a small area for a short time. Because the usual signs of status and wealth are absent, the social barriers that separate people under other circumstances disappear. There is no way of knowing

Suttons Bay

whether those on small boats made their purchase by choice or because of cash limitations. Likewise, owners of large boats may have made their purchase with excess cash or they may have a loan that looks like the national debt. In addition, among boaters, dressing down is almost a religion with its basic tenet being "less is more." Depending on your philosophy as well as your pocketbook, however, the amount spent on casual apparel can be more rather than less. But whether boutique or outlet shopper, it is usually difficult to identify the multimillionaires from those worrying about their next boat loan payment simply from their manner of dress. This has led many posh harbor restaurants to relax their dress requirements to a mere "shoes and shirt required."

People seem to take on a different persona when they board their boats. They appear to lose their concern with living up to preconceived images of themselves and become more comfortable just being who they are. Once on their boat, it is as if they leave behind the rules that govern their behavior at home. The compulsive house cleaner may find it unnecessary to tidy up the boat while the mess-maker at home washes and tidies the boat compulsively. A person stymied by a clogged drain at home may learn to replace the boat's entire freshwater system and one who couldn't boil an egg in a huge kitchen at home may learn to cook gourmet meals in space equivalent to their home's kitchen closet.

Literally and figuratively, time on a boat brings family members closer together. Having to contend with each other in close quarters on a daily basis changes family dynamics. The needs of each family member become equally important because there is nowhere to escape from one another. People tend to be a little more sensitive to one another's needs than they are at home. They are slower to anger and more indulgent of each other. Even spouses tend to go out of their way to avoid irritating each other. Children pitch in with daily tasks more

Charlevoix

willingly and parents tend to give them responsibilities and privileges beyond those they have at home. We spoke with one father who, in spite of his doubts, allowed his teenage son and his son's friend to take his sailboat out of the slip, through the channel, and raise the sails without his advice or interference. In doing so, he probably gained more respect for his offspring and is more likely to trust him to accomplish other tasks. In return, his child is likely to gain more self-confidence and respect for his father. Spending time on a boat together does not make dysfunctional families into healthy, cohesive units, but people do seem to be a bit nicer to one another. Occasionally, positive attitude changes do spill over to the home setting. Any activity that can accomplish such a feat has a great deal to say for it.

The social life in a harbor is very different from one in a land-based community, primarily in intensity. When boaters meet, they immediately have something in common. Because they know such meetings may be transitory, there is an urgency to maximize the quality and quantity of time spent together. There are therefore numerous planned and impromptu gatherings in any harbor on any day. These may be as informal as the crews from two boats putting their respective groceries together for a shared barbecue or as formal as a three-day rendezvous for 50 boats planned a year in advance. Some of the impromptu gatherings start simply with casual conversation among folks with adjoining dock slips. Others begin when someone hangs out a party flag which is an invitation to come on board for any boater who sees it. Planned events usually occur on weekends. Sponsors of these may be the local harbor administration, an employer, a boat club, or may simply be a planned gathering of old friends. The kind, size, and length of the social events are only as limited as the enthusiasm and planning efforts of the participants.

Ludington

Charlevoix

He reads
To her, but it's
He who loves to go where
Good guys win and no mistake is
Fatal

Charlevoix

In the harbors, relationships between boaters and towns-people are often as good as they are among boaters. One story told to us by a gentleman from Chicago is a dramatic demonstration. He and his wife had cruised to a small Michigan harbor and were relaxing on deck when she was stung by a bee. Her husband yelled for help when she began having an intense allergic reaction and had difficulty breathing. Neighboring boaters at the dock called 911 and a helicopter was immediately sent to transport her to a hospital. The town's sheriff rushed to the dock and transported the gentleman to the hospital where the sheriff waited with him. When his wife was released, the sheriff took the couple to the drugstore to fill prescriptions received at the hospital and returned them to their boat. The gentleman thought that the response he received in this harbor community, a place where he was a transient and knew no one, was probably better than he would have received at home.

Serious boaters spend a large portion of their spare time and vacations on board partially because they simply love it and partially because of the rather significant monetary investment involved. Time not spent cruising is often spent trying to learn more about boats and boating or preparing the boat for a cruise. Seamanship requires the understanding and eventual mastery of such diverse subjects as maintenance, safety, navigation, weather, electronics, rules of the road, and boat handling. In just one small popular handbook, there are 11 chapters with coverage of subjects as diverse as how to give CPR, docking techniques, how to use electronic navigating devices, and what kind of oil to use in your engine. Beyond a plethora of "how-to" books, there are numerous courses available. The U.S. Power Squadrons, the U.S. Coast Guard Auxiliary, and the American Red Cross offer free courses in piloting and seamanship. Frequently, the weekend boater will spend weekday evenings preparing the boat so that weekends can be spent on the water. Especially for boaters on the Great Lakes, the time available to be on the water is too brief to allow too much of it to be spent in repairs or preparation. Maximizing your time on the water can take much planning and organization. At one of the more crowded urban marinas, one family told us they arrive early Friday evening, put everything on board, get fuel so they avoid the long Saturday morning lines, and sleep on board overnight so they can get an early morning start.

Where boaters go, so go their pets. Whether they be dogs, cats, birds, rodents, or reptiles, many owners refuse to leave them at home in spite of the problems created by having them on board. Some owners say either they cannot arrange for or, in some cases, afford absentee pet care. In most cases, pets are simply an integral part of the family. The number, kind, and personality of the pets may actually determine the size and kind of boat the owner will purchase. One would-be sailor we met opted for a power boat due to an aging pet's inability to adapt to the narrow decks of a sailboat.

Dogs appear to be the most popular animal crew members. They come in every conceivable size, not infrequently in multiples. Three large dogs, two children, and two adults aboard a 35-foot sloop was the maximum population this writer encountered. In many cases, dogs function as more than just company, for they frequently act like an alarm system when the crew is onboard. When the crew is away from the boat, a dog can discourage uninvited visitors. Often, a dog who is everyone's pal when on the dock, is so protective as to be unapproachable by all but family members when onboard. Due to their popularity, most marinas provide special areas in which to walk dogs. There are even some more affluent marinas that provide dispensers with disposable plastic gloves for cleaning up after canine boaters. Concern for a pet's safety has meant that many a dog must tolerate the

Petosky

safety vests their owners insist they wear. And the observer must not assume that a sailboat with mesh nets strung around the bow rails has young children onboard. It may be there solely to protect the canine passengers.

Casual passersby see cats on deck less frequently than dogs since cats rarely enjoy an audience. The mariner cat is usually quite content to snooze in the sun within the protective confines of the cabin. They tolerate life on board, but some only barely. Unlike a dog, they do not like to expose their noses or fur to the wind and, although more agile than dogs, prefer a prone position when the boat is underway. Cats can be great companions on board, but normally only at dockside. Having a cat rather than a dog on your boat has the same major advantage that exists in a house; it needn't be walked. In addition to rarely appearing on deck, a cat is not likely to willingly go for a swim, so safety vests are not normally a dress requirement for feline first mates.

Boaters are independent human beings with vastly different personalities, passions, and lifestyles. It is possible, however, to observe and identify certain groups among them. There are the *runners* and the *absorbers*. The runners spend an afternoon or evening in a harbor and then run to the next. The absorbers settle into a harbor and stay until they must go home or until they think they have seen and done everything the harbor has to offer. There are the *stay-at-homes* and the *adventurers*. The stay-at-homes will not go out on the big lakes unless water and weather conditions are absolutely perfect and, even then, rarely venture far from their home port. The adventurer looks to travel to places never seen and will risk less-than-perfect conditions. The adventurer is not necessarily one of another group: the *foolhardy*. The foolhardy go cruising in any weather condition regardless of the limitations of their skill or their boat. This is a small group, however, since its members tend to leave its ranks after their first really

Bay Harbor

East Tawas

Detroit

frightening experience. There are the *enthusiasts* who leave the harbor for the "big water" as soon as provisions are onboard and who stay out for as long as those provisions last. (It is difficult for the full-time worker to be part of this group.) In contrast are the *parade watchers* who rarely ever move their boats from their slips. The latter may spend their days on deck ensconced in a comfortable chair, feet up, under an umbrella or not, watching the enthusiasts come and go. Some boaters come to the harbor straight from work, suits still on, and briefcases in hand. These folks do not pack and unpack; they keep an alternative wardrobe onboard. Some of these boaters are simply *time savers*, while others fall into the *I-love-my work-and-everything-will-stop-without-me* category (known more commonly as workaholics). There was a time when a workaholic would not have considered purchasing a boat. The advent of computers and cellular phones allowed many in this group to become boat owners because they could mix work and pleasure, with a heavy accent on the work. In contrast to the last group are those in the *I-must-have-my-space-or-I'll-go-crazy* group who will not allow business to interfere with boating. And a group too large to omit is made up of those people who go boating only so they can fish (the *I-boat-to-fish* group). Some of their guests and crew, however, use fishing as a reason to be on the boat (the *I-fish-to-boat* group).

Contrary to what many non-boat-owners believe, people who own boats are not all wealthy. Many people whose dream it is to own a boat, buy an old one and take a few years to restore it. Some save specifically to buy one. Others who may have considered buying a cottage reason that a boat has an equivalent cost, will allow them to see different places and meet a lot of new people, and has no grass to mow. Some people who either cannot manage the costs by themselves or who know they will only occasionally use it, buy a boat with partners much like a condominium time-share arrangement. A growing number of people retire, sell their homes, and live on their boats. Some have dreams of world travel, some move with the seasons between their home port and one in warmer climes, and some move where their whims take them. Occasionally, some must stop and go back to work for short periods to revitalize their coffers. One couple we met had sold their farm, but did not want to leave Michigan, so they move between their boat and an inexpensive trailer home. There are a very lucky few who have the use of a relative's boat or have received one as an inheritance. Probably the largest number of boaters with whom we have spoken take much of the income they have for entertainment and luxuries and spend it on their boat and the boating lifestyle.

Boaters express their differences by the nature of their boats or the gear on them. The most obvious, beyond size, are the differences between sailors and power boaters. Traditionally, these two groups had very little to do with one another. There was a certain snobbery expressed by sailors because they felt that sailing was somehow more challenging and less dependent on fuel than was power boating. This feeling has diminished tremendously in the face of automation and the nature of modern day cruising. Sailboats may now be equipped with an automatic pilot, radar, airconditioning, roller furling, and power windlasses. Sailors who once left from and returned to their docks under sail, now do so under power because harbor crowding and narrow channels do not allow for the maneuvers one must make while under sail. This means dependency on fuel. Also, today's lifestyle dictates that one must get from point A to point B in a defined time. Your client or boss is not likely to be pleased to hear you did not make it to work because there wasn't enough wind.

There are other things about boaters' choices of boats that occasionally separates them. There is a group whose boats are built for speed, but they don't race. Anothers' are built for

Leland

Lake Erie Metropark

Frankfort

Port Sanilac

speed and they race whenever possible. There is a third group whose boats are built only for cruising, but they occasionally race although they don't know why they bother. Members of the first group are considered speed demons by the other two. Occasionally a speed demon is transformed into a racer, but racers rarely become speed demons. Racers cannot imagine why you would get on a boat to do anything but race. As they age, however, they are frequently transformed into cruisers. New cruisers are occasionally bitten by either the speed or racing bug and have been known to sell a boat after a season or two in order to satisfy their new passion. Folks who have cruised for a long time, however, are rarely transformed.

Another "separator" is whether or not a boat has all the most modern electronics on board...and whether or not the skipper has become totally dependent upon them (or even knows how to use them!). Many of those who have electronic navigation aids think those who resist installing such devices are stubbornly foolish or simply old-fashioned. There are those, however, who have resisted electronics due to the cost of purchase and installation. (Some with sailboats and no electronics, fearing they present too small a target to be visible on another boat's radar, fly radar reflectors to assure they will be seen by others in the fog.) Those who are totally dependent on their electronics are frequently criticized by both the seat-of-their-pants navigators and those who use the electronic aids but can navigate without them. This criticism stems from the concern that a captain who does not know how to navigate without electronics may put himself and his crew at risk if his electronics should fail. In addition, the other two groups know they may be called on to rescue a boat with such a captain which may put them at risk if weather conditions are severe. With the numerous potential divisions that exist among boaters, it is amazing that the things they have in common usually eclipse their differences.

But no one, with the possible exclusion of teenagers, wants to have too many things in common. Since boats lined up at a pier are much like a row of apartment houses or suburban homes—different from each other but only in subtle ways—boaters frequently decorate their boats. Some use bold strokes whereas others are more content with minor statements of individuality. There are boats that appear to have their own botanical gardens aboard while others have one artificial plant in the cabin's window. Some boat interiors have the look of an elaborate wood-paneled library from a Victorian mansion, some look like floating naval antique stores, while some mimic the sterility of an operating room. The decorations that boaters use may include paintings, carvings, stuffed animals, or plaques with witty or inspirational messages. The methods used to personalize a boat's interior are as endless as the owner's imagination and pocketbook. By flying flags, boaters subtly announce to others who they are: a University of Michigan graduate, a Michigan State University supporter, a member of a specific yacht club, or simply a skipper who loves a party and has the cocktail flag to prove it. Perhaps they do this as much in the hopes of finding people of like interests as it is to identify themselves. A boat's name may tell something about the owners, but perhaps that should be the subject of another book.

We all like to personalize the places to which we return, even if we only rent them for a season. To this end, boaters may decorate the docks where they have their slip with such items as wind chimes, planters, weather vanes, flags, kites, and mailboxes. In many harbors, there appears to be a new art form: the intricate weaving of dock lines into geometric arrays. There was a time when it was sufficient to efficiently secure your boat to the dock with white or naturally colored lines. You then left these on the dock in such a way that no one would trip on them, but they would be instantly available if needed.

Caseville

Now, walking up and down the dock feels a little like a visit to an art fair. Dock lines come in a rainbow of colors which many boaters select to contrast with or match the decor of their boats. The creative patterns into which the ropes are coiled and braided are fascinating. It seems a shame that these works of art are so temporal and that they are destroyed when the boat leaves the dock. Perhaps these dock line artists have something in common with ice and sand sculptors whose work lasts only a short time.

Although there are those who think docks already provide too many conveniences, some feel further elaboration is needed. These boaters, especially those renting slips long-term, have been known to add such accessories to their dock space as a satellite dish, freestanding steps to provide easier access to bigger boats, a dockbox or cooler, and even a special water filtration unit through which the water provided at dockside flows before reaching the boat.

For boaters, a dock is merely their front yard. When a boater enters a slip, the dock complex immediately surrounding them is their temporary neighborhood; the harbor beyond, their temporary hometown. It is more than simply being on a boat that draws millions to cruise the Great Lakes. It is also the excitement of having the variety of experiences available in a kaleidoscope of hometowns.

Rogers City

65

Sebawaing

East Jordan

Tawas

South Haven

We learned
The rules and how
Not to feel, we built our
Walls and now watch the children with
Envy.

Caseville

I'll rise
To the challenge
Of open waters, man,
Against wind and waves, right after
My nap.

Traverse City

Oscoda

Presque Isle

Detroit

Detroit

Traverse City

Slick black
Torpedoes stand
Ready for battle with
Docks that threaten the boat's perfect
White shell.

Holland

Harbor Beach

Mt. Clemens

Presque Isle

Harrisville

Frankfort

Leland

Rigid.
Flash frozen, the
Flowing spectrum of blue
Is stilled; its brilliance preserved for
Spring's thaw.

Charlevoix

Portage Lake

Greilickville

Caseville

Mackinaw City

Port Sanilac

Port Huron

Portage Lake

Safe harbors are not simply places to which boaters retreat from the open waters of the lake. They are the hubs of activity where the dividing lines between the town and townspeople, boats and boaters, and tourist attractions and tourists become blurred. The complex interaction that results from the input of each of these factions creates what C.J. and I call the harbor experience.

Each harbor of Michigan's Lower Peninsula has a distinctive character. Some are sheltered from the waters of a Great Lake only by man-made breakwalls. Some harbors are on river channels close to a river's mouth while others are as much as seven miles upstream. Access to a harbor may merely require going through a short channel or it may require waiting until a swinging railroad bridge is moved or a drawbridge is raised. Some harbors are large and deep; others are small and shallow. Even the breakwalls are different. They may be made of rock, concrete, or metal. They may have walkways and railings so boaters can get a land's-eye view of the harbor or they may be suitable only for nesting gulls. Harbors may be tranquil and remote, located in busy tourist towns, or be part of a city's downtown landscape. Some ports appeal more to those who love to fish and others to those seeking a quaint, old-town atmosphere. Some harbors are known for their selection of good restaurants or shops, some for their diversions for young children, some for their nearby beaches, some for their natural beauty. It is the very diversity of the harbors that makes cruising along Michigan's shoreline so appealing.

In spite of harbors' differences, some things are constant. Each has a place, either at a breakwall or channel entrance, where you sense the safety of the harbor begins. The wind dies down and the resistance of the water against the hull diminishes.

Inside the harbor, regardless of its location, there are images and sounds that are essential parts of the *harbor experience*. They are so familiar to boaters that, frequently, they register only on a subconscious level: the macramé patterns of coiled ropes, the laser light show projected onto the sides of boats by sunlight bouncing off the water, the regular geometry of wood planking, the abstract lines of wood grains, the line drawings made by crowded masts against a blank blue sky, and the starbursts that leap from chrome lit by direct sunlight.

The sounds are many. Birds lend their distinctive voices to the harbor's subdued din: the throaty click of the swallows, the raucous scream of the gulls, the high shrill call of the sandpipers, and the insistent, nasal quacking of female mallards as they try to keep their young from straying. Of the myriad noises and rhythms in the harbor, some are soothing; others carry undertones of anxiety. The gentle slap of water against the hull at dockside speaks of quiet waters. The creaking of the dock lines is reassuring, a comforting sound that says you are safe, attached, secure. In contrast, the staccato snapping of flags in the wind speaks of the imminent potential for foul weather and the fog horn's sound causes all who hear it to take heed. The sound of rain on the deck sends a universal message to boaters who have hatches to close and cockpits to cover before retreating below for shelter and amusement.

Even in bad weather, there is little you can do at home that you cannot do in a marina. Dockside services frequently include fresh water, power, and cable TV, and most marinas have their own laundry and shower facilities, picnic tables, grills, and areas in which to walk your dog. There are always fuel pumps and pump-out facilities, since it is against the law to pump waste overboard. In some of the harbors more popular with those who fish, there are elaborate fish cleaning facilities. These include inclined stainless steel tables for easy washing, water hoses with spray nozzles that hang in

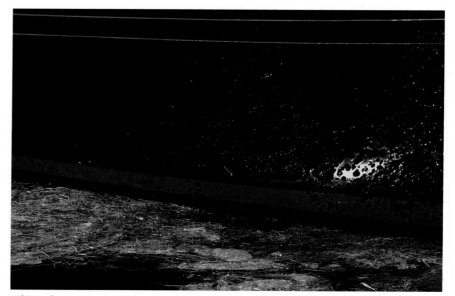

White Lake

readiness, and electric grinders beneath the table for the left-overs.

Changing technology has brought, and will continue to bring, new conveniences and services to the docks, marinas, and harbors. What technology cannot do is guarantee you a reservation for a boat slip. However, cellular phone technology has made it easier to make a reservation for dock space before you ever reach the harbor.

The harbor is birthplace and home or, at least, hunting grounds for a wide assortment of birds. Most hunters are merely transients, coming in to fish or catch insects: Black and Caspian terns, Great Blue and Green-Backed herons, and an assortment of plovers and sandpipers to name but a few. Those that make the harbor home and breeding ground are alternately loved and shunned by the humans with whom they share the space. Almost without exception, children greet with enthusiasm the Canada geese, the mallards, the ring-billed gulls, and the swans. While adults enjoy watching them and find the goslings and ducklings delightful, the need to scrape their droppings from swim platforms, dinghies, and meticulously groomed decks has given many a nature lover a reason to make their love conditional. Displays of owls or coiled snakes reflect the last desperate measures of skippers overburdened by the unwanted attention of local birds. The accumulation of large numbers of birds can be dangerous because their excretions can foul the water of the harbor so that swimming is a health hazard for humans. In some harbors, signs are posted to discourage people from feeding the birds. Not only does this avoid encouraging large numbers of birds from accumulating, it keeps them from becoming too aggressive and too dependent on people.

Some of the smaller birds that breed in the harbors perform us a service. The barn and cliff swallows are enthusiastic insect eaters, flying around with mouths open wide, scooping

Harbor Beach

up as many insects as they are able. Humans have done these birds a service by building docks with structures that double as convenient nesting places. At a number of harbors, the cliff swallows make their mud nests beneath the metal canopies of pier lights in groups of up to nine. Looking like spokes of an umbrella beneath the metal lamp shades, each burrow may have an adult swallow peering out from its opening. When walking beneath these burrows, human passersby should be cautious because birds know not to foul their sleeping quarters. To this end, they stick their tail feathers out of their mud burrows far enough to make sure their deposits land beyond the nest and on the dock below.

Bird stories abound among boaters. One skipper told us of the time he was crossing from Wisconsin to Michigan when a dense fog overtook his boat. Suddenly, small birds covered his sailboat as well as the shoulders and heads of the crew. After a short time, they were gone as suddenly as they arrived. Perhaps a flock of migrating birds just needed a rest. One family told us of coming to their slip for their first outing of the summer only to find a mallard nesting on their swimming platform. Did they dispossess Mama Mallard? On the contrary, they delayed their voyage until the young went for their first swim.

Because most crew members cannot live by cable TV and reading matter alone, once dockside many quickly seek other diversions. And so harbors become much more than places to find shelter and fuel. They become places to shop, to eat, to be entertained, and to find others with whom to pursue these pleasures.

Visitors who anticipate ranging farther afield typically come prepared with bikes, roller blades or even mopeds and power scooters. (I have even observed a fullsized amphibious automobile being lowered over the side of a large yacht.) Bicycles seem to be the most popular choice for land transport, perhaps because they are available with so many options. For easier

New Buffalo

carrying and stowing, some fold into carrying bags no larger in diameter than one wheel. Stainless steel and aluminum models are popular since they can take a season's dousing without rusting. If desired, you can even buy a bicycle in a color that will match your boat's decor. Sometimes this shoreside transportation is a diversion in itself. At other times, it is carried because there are specific destinations to reach. For those who prefer to keep their onboard gear pared down, more and more ports offer bike rental services.

Each harbor has its particular attractions. Extremely popular destinations in some harbors are the marvelous neighboring swimming beaches. These are especially attractive to parents who want to do something they can enjoy and still keep young children and/or teenagers amused. Frequently, harbors with nice waterfronts or good beaches offer an abundance of free entertainment throughout the summer months to attract more boaters. Often, there are offerings of festivals, parades, and street fairs. Good fishing is the main requirement for some. There are a number of harbors that have tailored their stores and physical facilities to keep fisherpersons happy. There are harbors with special biking and roller-blading paths, and some ports are a must for boaters who do not cruise without their golf clubs. Harbors with a number of golf courses nearby are, of course, on the top of link-lovers' must-stop places. And if the movies that are showing in town are not to the liking of the crew, there are usually plentiful video rental stores for those with the foresight to have a VCR onboard. Other marvelous destinations are the state parks, some of which may be within biking distance of the harbor.

There are a number of harbors that appear to have been designed with the dedicated shopper in mind. It is amazing how many different shops can be crammed into a main street that may be no more than five blocks long. Boutiques and galleries abound. There may be several bookstores scattered among

Traverse City

Port Sanilac

Charlevoix

these with the occasional specialty coffee shop next door. But perhaps the one interest group successfully serviced by the greatest number of harbors are the "diners." Restaurants of all sizes and with a variety of food specialties and price ranges have flourished in the harbors to attract this very large segment of the boating public. Regardless of how many varied and exotic provisions there may be onboard, eating out is usually the preferred option.

As a result of all this development, many harbors attract the nonboating tourist population as well. Some towns with winter populations in the hundreds swell to a summer count of several, or many, thousands. Although this does wonders for local economies, there is often a downside. In season, harbors face many of the same problems that cities have year-round. They must resolve how to handle trash and sewage disposal, provide power and water, and make and enforce rules. Some of the rules are simple: no bike-riding or roller-skating on the docks, walk dogs only in designated areas, lights and noise must be below the level that would disturb neighbors after a certain time, and, in some areas, no fishing. Much of the enforcement is left to the boaters themselves with the dockmaster as a sort of referee. There is, however, the occasional need for more serious law enforcement which is provided by the sheriff, conservation officer, coast guard, or even the border patrol. One or more of these usually maintain a presence in the harbors.

Harbor communities must decide when and which facilities to build, expand, or replace. Financial support for the facilities is derived primarily from fees boaters pay for upkeep and operation of docks, piers, showers, restrooms, and other local facilities at the harbor. The state steps in only when local support is not sufficient. In 1996, the state operated only 13 of Michigan's harbors. The local municipal government has jurisdiction over most public marinas so harbor management is an integral part of local politics. Depending on the sentiments

Saugatuck

Northport

of the townspeople and who they elect from year to year, the marinas and harbor may receive more or less attention and funding. Most boaters are blissfully ignorant of these subtle influences because most are present for a comparatively short time each year. Only those who have leased dock space in one marina over several years and who consistently interact with the townspeople tend to become aware and interested in how local politics impacts their temporary homes.

There are those who might claim that a temporary home is an oxymoron. For many, home has little to do with the location or the physical nature of the shelter. Rather, it is simply wherever our loved ones happen to be. Whether a harbor is a boater's temporary home or simply a momentary stopping place, the harbors are places with a strange mixture of camaraderie and competition, cooperation and one-up-manship, frantic entertainment and relaxation, and adventure and security. The harbors are the safety net that gives many a boater the confidence to venture onto the bigger waters beyond.

It makes little difference whether there are more boaters because of the increased numbers of safe harbors or whether the increasing number of boaters drives the need for more safe harbors. The fact is that the harbors are a growing string of communities that provide even the landlubber with a plethora of pleasures. These little communities on the shorelines of our country represent a growing part of our nation's economy for, in them, boaters and tourists spend more and more money every year. But beyond all the pleasures and the business of boating and tourism, we all like knowing that somewhere we can always find a safe harbor.

Lake Erie Metropark

Pentwater

Elk Rapids

Harbor Springs

Presque Isle

White Lake

Leland

Leland

Grand Haven

Suttons Bay

St. Clair Shores

Leland

South Haven

Holland

Portage Lake

South Haven

Petosky

I wish
My window on
Adventure was not one
That required I scrub it with
A mop.

Northport

Lake Erie Metropark

The race
Is not over
When the boat reaches port.
The manner of transport simply
Changes.

South Haven

Harbor Springs

Cheboygan County

Saugatuck

East Tawas

Port Sanilac

Harbor Beach

Ludington

St. Joseph

Ludington

Boyne City

If I
Should lean on you,
I'll do it, not to keep
From falling, but because I love
Your warmth.

Elk Rapids

Northport

To roam
And wonder in
The harbors of the world
Is the boaters' special kind of
Freedom.

East Tawas